Trumpets in the Sky

Trumpets in the Sky

poems by Jerry Garcia

~ 2022 ~

Trumpets in the Sky
© Copyright 2022 Jerry Garcia
All rights reserved. No part of this book may be used or reproduced in any manner whatsoever without written permission from either the author or the publisher, except in the case of credited epigraphs or brief quotations embedded in articles or reviews.

Editor-in-chief
Eric Morago

Editor Emeritus
Michael Miller

Marketing Specialist
Ellen Webre

Proofreader
Jim Hoggatt

Front cover art
Émile-Antoine Bayard's wood engraving for Around the Moon by Jules Verne (1870)

Author photo
Ajay Jhaveri

Book design
Michael Wada

Moon Tide logo design
Abraham Gomez

Trumpets in the Sky
is published by Moon Tide Press

Moon Tide Press
6709 Washington Ave. #9297
Whittier, CA 90608
www.moontidepress.com

FIRST EDITION

Printed in the United States of America

ISBN # 978-1-7350378-9-9

More Praise for *Trumpets in the Sky*

In this collection, Jerry Garcia describes breath rising from a body in "leftover incandescence." I can think of no more apt metaphor for these poems — they are shimmering and ragged, full of cosmic wonder and exhaustion. There are birds but also cars, galaxies and suburbs, pills and cubicles and Hawaii. The language startles. The pace avalanches. "I come to agitate your day" Garcia says, early on. But for all his quick mind, by the end of the volume he admits, "I am not the salvation the world needs / that once I thought I could be." This book trumpets poems for tired souls who choose transcendence over surrender. A book not to change the world, but to unlock galaxies inside. Garcia writes: "let our joints resolve / into one heavy piece of the universe." How does he capture so much weight and light at once?

— Brian Sonia-Wallace, Poet Laureate of West Hollywood, Author of *The Poetry of Strangers*

Jerry Garcia's poems are both a celebration and a lament, a generational songbook noting the everyday and the not-quite mythic. "I am hunger on the run..." he declares in poems teeming with irony, sensuality and melancholy. A Southern California landscape is both a Golden Land and a wasteland, where "...the often-grungy flatlands/sparkle like a box of jewels" and where the streets of Nichols Canyon are a "roadside canvas." Ironically summoning a beat aesthetic and a surrealist imagination, García stays in the inescapable, imperfect present, where joy has meaning and beauty because of what has been lost or is fading.

— Ramón García, Ph.D., *The Chronicles*

Blaring title, yes, and yet I'm most drawn to the quiet of fine human observations, the still and meaningful realism, the visceral musings through which Jerry Garcia seeks to "illuminate this mood of apprehension" suffusing our world. I'm most moved by his persistent focus on the humane, "whittled from a life of misread instructions." I can feel hope, "like a silk sheet weighted with sugar and salt," call to me, pulse for me, enfold me, "tuning and retuning in service of unfinished songs."

— Peter J. Harris, author, *Bless the Ashes & Black Man of Happiness: In Pursuit of My 'Unalienable Right'*

For Becky

Contents

Foreword by Beth Ruscio   10
Preface   12

Trumpets in the Sky   17
Are You Flying Tonight?   18
Human Touch   19
All That Is Left of the Rain   21
Suddenly a Storm   22
When We Endorse the Noise of Conflagration   23
From Dawn to Dusk   25
On the Night the Stars Collapse   27
Dog Years   28
Oranges   29
A Loser Flexes on Pathology Street   30
Espresso   31
Kids with Sides   32
Gargoyle Clinging to Weakened Towers   33
Oceanic Worship   34
Round-Shouldered Dreadnought   35
Two Doves Alight on a Dead Walnut Tree   36
Under a Murders' Watch   38
Radiance   39
Blankets or Dark   40
Orange Horizon Capped Blue at Sunset   41
Schwinn Cruiser   42
Nichols Canyon   44
Railroad Ties   45
Email from the Dead   46
Thunder Clash Nightmare   47
Eyes   48
Rainy Afternoon Music: Carly Simon/Abraxas, 1972   49
After *Invasion of the Body Snatchers*   51
Downwind from a Man Sleeping in His Own Puddle   52
Singing Half-Songs by the Sea   53
Tempest   54
Hitchhiking Through Fire and Rain   55
Contrition   56
Journeys   57

Storms of Change, Squalls of Pestilence	59
Hawaiian Urban Dusk	60
Slack Key	61
I Guess It's Too Late to Be a Major League Baseball Player	62
I Found My Friend Richard in a Painting from the 17th Century	63
Lost in Space	64
The Cleanliness of Sand	65
Gestures, Situations, and Surveillances	66
Venus-Moon Conjunction	67
Dawn Broke Time Makes Two	69
The Deep Heart's Core	71
Rainy Night House	72
There Was Never Enough Exposure to Shoot Your Moon	73
A Plunge Through Ozone	74
ePoem	75
Starling's Triumphant Flight	76
Whiter Than Pale	78
While Walking the Dog Last Evening	79
Floating	80
About the Author	*82*
Author's Notes	*83*
Acknowledgements	*86*

Foreword

'A bright-eyed melancholy' is the first note I made on *Trumpets in the Sky*. This describes both the work, and its author—consider his endearingly named website: www.gratefulnotdead.com, which both winks at the joke, and adds a dollop of relief. Yep, still here.

In the wonder years of this new century, I first saw Jerry Garcia one Sunday morning in the Silverlake apartment where Laurel Ann Bogen held her private poetry workshop. At that hour, in the living room, on the shadowy side of the building, dimly illuminated by, let's call it, brothel lighting, we gathered. The recorded voice of a poet reading their work played over the speakers. It was the ritual beginning that as a theater artist and a lapsed Catholic to boot suited me just fine and made the moody morning feel like communion as we listened, and watched each other listen, to great poetry. Later, on the sidewalk in the jolting wattage of Southern California's everybody-else-has-gone-surfin' afternoon, I got a good look at Jerry. I don't believe I caught his last name until months later, but our enduring friendship began outside, where sometimes for as long as the workshop, we replayed the morning's work, hashing over the fine points, both of us reluctant to let go of the spell that poetry had cast over us. Then, we discovered, we had the so-called universal language of cinema in common—each of us had logged countless hours working around cameras, he behind them, me in front. Even as new friends, we talked like old friends.

In this same disarming way, this book feels like an open invitation to be his sidekick, to be a party to his travels. The road is definitely a recurring theme in Jerry's work—his earlier collections, *Hitchhiking with the Guilty* and *On Summer Solstice Road*, testify to that romance, "I am hunger on the run." Although, like all the best seekers, he's less enchanted with arriving because after a little hand holding, he just "might be attached to a comet hurtling through a galaxy." As ballast for these many outward-bound journeys, including trips that never leave the sacred spot of his own living room, he delivers the constant hum of engagement with both the strange and the mundane. Jerry wears his sense of wonder like a favorite hat. This is writing tempered by a hard-won acceptance of taking the world on its own terms "at the Eucharist line of bliss and decadence." There's confession in this book. There's tenderness, lots of it, doling it out toward loved ones, toward strangers, and maybe, in the most unsentimental way, to Japhy Ryder, the dog he named after a character in "Dharma Bums." It fits—the cadence of his inquiries, the up and down beats of what he brings to the page, imagining a jazz pianist improvising underneath. To be in the company of these poems is to see a world through a lens that's composing a shot like a portrait, taking in the fleeting, the lasting, moments small and large, the wow's and the how about that's. Jerry is that rare combination: thoughtful, generous, an easy laugher, a serious man. And I think with this book, he's given his passions free reign, to quote Kerouac, like "the Japhies of the world . . . to find the ecstasy of the stars, to find the dark mysterious secret of the origin of faceless wonderless crapulous civilization." Read all about it.

—Beth Ruscio, author of *Speaking Parts*

Preface

On a Sunday afternoon, I was driving east on one of those infamous interconnecting freeways near the Los Angeles Civic Center. Above the cityscape something caught my eye. A huge airliner revealed itself from behind a great cloud as sun glistened on its silver exterior. I pointed it out to my wife, Becky, who was reading the news on her mobile phone. By the time she found where I was pointing, the plane had disappeared behind a cluster of buildings.

"You should have seen it," I told her with the enthusiasm of an eight-year-old boy. She wasn't all that interested in what—to her—would have been a mundane sight. As she returned to the news, she nonchalantly said: "You're always fascinated by things in the sky."

And with that, a title was born. "Things in the Sky" eventually became "Trumpets in the Sky," because trumpets sound with proclamation as I hope these poems do.

Not all the poems involve things in the firmament. Some are meant to echo our collective fears, hits, misses, and yearnings we share. There is a revised version of a prescient piece that didn't have a subject until after we had buried my mother.

In 7th grade, I was introduced to poetry by a spunky nun named Sister Martina, who sparked an interest that would last me a lifetime. In high school, Mr. J.D. Hokoyama and a Jesuit named Gordon Bennet introduced me to literature. Mixed in with Updike and Salinger were Keats, Bryant, and E.E. Cummings. As my formative years were between 1967 and 1972, the singer-songwriter pantheon of Bob Dylan, Joni Mitchell, Leonard Cohen, Jackson Browne, and Hoyt Axton made the construction of lyrical phrases practical to me. In college, I received encouragement from the departed novelist, Carolyn See, who noticed early poetry in my class journal.

It would take another 25 years before I made a serious stab at writing poetry. In the late 1990s I studied with Laurel Ann Bogen, treasured SoCal poet and teacher. A few of the poems in this book were conceived in her master class. Michael C Ford became another mentor with whom I "wood-shedded" a number of these pages. Gratitude goes to Beth Ruscio for her foreword and friendship. Thanks to another important poetry friend and multimedia collaborator, E. Amato, who helped me with commas and periods. She also contributed to my work by shearing confusion from some hastily written verse. I thank Eric Morago and Moon Tide Press for helping this work see the light of day. But foremost, I thank my wife Becky for inspiration that goes beyond the title "Trumpets in the Sky."

"You are an aperture through which the universe is looking at and exploring itself."

— Alan Watts

"There was nowhere to go but everywhere, so just keep on rolling under the stars."

— Jack Kerouac

Trumpets in the Sky

Through scattered clouds, pink and thin,
silver jets spark yearnings for adventure.
Powerlines scratch black strokes on cobalt.
The full glide of a Cooper's Hawk
casts gray shadows
before talons hook wire.

A bluff-side turns orange with twilight.
Lovers' hands silhouette in promise,
as the last remaining sunrays mute.
Distant aircraft reflect the blaze
of further western time zones.
Late for home, sparrows bullet toward shelter.

Incandescent fragments open across the valley.
Neon signs glow on street travelers
riding roadsters.

Outlines of passion grow opaque
against evening firmament.
Diamond stars dress
the blue-black curtain
that introduces
the obvious
moon.

Are You Flying Tonight?

Jet engines strain to gain lift
whining like a holiday pinwheel
and I wonder if you are the pilot.

For so long, you were the lens on my camera.
Together we twisted focus.

You added the filter; I measured the light.

But now an automatic switch
makes it easy for me to snap a view.

I watch your flight through a long focal length
as your fuselage climbs
to a high angle through the clouds,
heading into the forever blue.

Human Touch

Headlights followed me
like a jet squadron in formation,
four lanes, eight lights
blurring from my exhaustion,
eyes reverting from rearview

to red glowing dots ahead,
when darkness came down
like a curtain drawn.
No lampposts, no cars,
no reflections.
Completely opaque,
like Sister Margaret Mary's story
about the world's end.

I became weightless,
a sprite in ocean air.
My vehicle no longer carried me.
I became awash in crashing waves.

The sea was black with white caps.
Was it moonlight or a patrolman's flashlight?
I might have been floating.
I might have been flying.
You found me in a hospital
"after days," you said.

I might have been in outer space
attempting inventory of countless stars
or maybe, they were specks of sand
at the bottom of the briny deep.

You didn't have a clue where I had gone,
but fed the dog and tended to the roses
while waiting.

You could be holding my hand right now.
Or I might be attached to a comet
hurtling through the galaxy,
long before the earth held water
or human touch came to be.

All That Is Left of the Rain

Cumulus clouds shadow
the eastern horizon,
hostile storms rumble forward
with the ferocity
of a Mahler symphony.

Under amber desk light,
I try to illuminate
this mood of apprehension.
I name it for that aerial display
outside my window.

Raindrops drum the rooftop
with discordant rhythms,
as if conducted by a distracted maestro.
None of my prompting
yields results sublime
as rainfall.

When tats and thumps
stop thrashing on the roof,
gray clouds glow
with the burn of blocked sun.

All that is left of the rain
is decomposition and thought.

Suddenly a Storm
April 2015

Freddie Gray rains pound
cotton-hooded men
on the drenched sidewalks
of Baltimore.
Strident walks turn to skirmishes
on the wet terrain.

Flowers continue to bloom
under opaque skies.
Televisions display
the contrary mess
of constabulary chauvinism.

Across the globe Mt Everest crumbles
as earthquakes panic
the people of Kathmandu.

Baltimore bottles up mayhem.
Nepal buries 9,000.
Cries echo under the rubble of hillsides
and the bite of fogging teargas.

All the while, a tuxedoed prom date preens
restless with strategies for his first fondle.
A father picks wet leaves
from his peeling porch.
Limousines flash color
on slick neighborhood asphalt.

Clouds encumber dusk,
but night-blooming jasmine says
Spring.

When We Endorse the Noise of Conflagration

In living room sanctuaries,
evening news repeats
washed-out images
of ancestral turbulence
in "shit-hole" countries.

On Main Street,
demonstrators carry torches
to proclaim their liberty
in a dogmatic battle between
founding-fathers' freedom and
the right to hate their neighbor.

Pepsi Light quenches our thirst,
as we watch swarms of protest
in faded pixels of satellite color.
In the absence of labels,
foreign zocalos renounce narcissism.

On inhabited hillsides
taste for hedonism
fuses sympathetic thoughts
with hot-tub spirituality.
The indulgences of leisure
block blighted images
of remote skirmishes.

Drums of sacrifice echo
from far-off mêlée
to battle hymns
of skinhead pride
through coast-to-coast
dinner time.

Not even the weather report
serves up equanimity
in these pandemic days.

Plastic in the wallet satisfies
temporal yearnings.
It clings to what importance
technology gleans.

Challenged by the indifference of avarice
the heart ignores its call to care
the mind does not create means
to follow distant struggles
or feed the hungry
across the street.

Turn off the TV
drink a cup of tea
in silence.

From Dawn to Dusk

Surfing on the tail of a comet
through inky cosmos
dodging space-trash
—rock, dust, and ice.
Hanging five
through atmospheres
of unknown globes
gesturing to ancient spheres
like friends on the shoreline.
Gliding easily in the quiet night
of space.

With an unsuspected jolt,
the devil himself claims
the comet's perch
pushing me off the tail.
Alone in a flat spin, I see the demagogue
riding my meteor like a chariot,
streaking clutter
through our galaxy,
hand raised in pontification,
screaming at the fire of the sun.

Shivering awake in a room
colored by liquid crystal.
3:30 in the morning red.
Sleep cut short with miles to go,
dreary tones play like cello
and bassoon, provocative at their pace,
performing to the inconsequential audience
of a man losing his wings
and falling back to earth.

Bleary-eyed waking hours, pissed-off, hungry.
Dreaded sense-memory conquering optimism.

On an automobile journey
through retail strips of vanishing industry
and auto repair shops,
grocery stores.
Leaving the flatlands
on winding roads toward a mythic city.
Tires roll over canyon dust,
dried bougainvillea scatters,
broken stems crackle under worn tires,
as sun rises over
the ridge that separates
jammed cityscape
from spacious suburbia.

It becomes a pristine day:
even the often-grungy flatlands
sparkle like a box of jewels.

On the Night the Stars Collapse

As our world compresses into stone,
fires undulate her rim
like a red remnant of coal.
I just want to feel you slide

over my body like a silk sheet
weighted with sugar and salt
splattered by tropical storms
warmed by spilling lava.

I just want to entwine our fingers,
knuckle to knuckle,
let our joints resolve
into one heavy piece of universe.

Dog Years

We don't talk much.
Japhy doesn't leave my side
except to be with my wife.
When she is in the bedroom
and I am in the den, he stretches
like a rug across the hallway.
A secret service agent watching
its charges, eyeing our every move.

Japhy, named for a Jack Kerouac
character, will someday be gone.

Waking me at 3:00 in the morning,
forgetting that he needs to pee, that
old man of a canine stands in the kitchen,
stares at the floor tile, his mind apparently lost.

I hold the door open, sniff for skunk.
Like an old jalopy, he restarts,
moving slowly over the threshold.

Coyotes jump fences when it is worthwhile.
Now I have become Japhy's guard.

When he returns, I offer the puppy treat he expects.
Once a ploy to suggest using the backyard as his potty,
15 years later, it has become our old couple's ritual.

Named for a Jack Kerouac character,
Japhy the dog will someday be gone.

Oranges

Don't misunderstand.
I remember most words
as I need them.
I can still drive a car with dexterity,
though I do misplace the keys
more often than not.

I found myself slicing an orange yesterday.
I used to love to peel.
A little starter knife would open the skin,
then fingernails separate the pulp
that binds the juicy fruit together.

With flesh and rind discarded,
I would pull apart each segment
and eat, sparingly, like special candies
from a box.

Seems like a lot of work for an impatient youth.
The irascible senior
chooses speed over art,
but for all the wisdom I once beheld,
I don't understand why.

A Loser Flexes on Pathology Street

Waiting for grit to congeal
to format a bone, a joint & limb
stand high above neglect
of a superior being's touch.
The swirling figure rises,
pint and blunt,
a tiny spoon sparkles white.

Super-colors of someone's brain
rain all over the shared sidewalk,
where the power greater
doles out good genes
with the luck of wind.

Dust becomes mandible
with the desire to talk.
But a clean body does not mean
sober thoughts.

Imagined crutches
dismantle and drag
against the wind.

The curtain closes.
Visions fade with time.

Comes the void.

Espresso

I live where trees grow from concrete,
where cars circle like cats
marking territory.
I wake to radio chatter,
take blood pressure medicine
from bottles next to the espresso maker
in my un-mopped kitchen.

One pill each:
blue flushes fluids,
orange slows the muscle's beat.
Blood flows
like a river of traffic
passing the logjams
of intersections.

Milk steamer pressure starts my day.
Thick espresso, a touch of froth.
Pistons pump under fragile tin hood,
as I stumble out the door—
laundry, papers, commuter cup in hand.

Driving a car too hot,
on a freeway too slow,
piles of worry
sit in a black briefcase
on black leather upholstery.
Cell phone compounds aggravation
with ex-wife's grumble.

Inside the carpark,
status is marked by location.
I disembark, my coffee
cold and bitter.

Through fluorescent corridors
of cubicles and machinery,
in the hallways of complaint,
charged and caffeinated,
I come to agitate your day.

Kids with Sides

Even the skinny guys
wear their shirt tails out
shirt-tailed stocky guys
still look fat.

On a sidewalk in Hollywood,
next to the Strasberg theater
actors, children really,
read "sides"
recite with emotion,
words written
for an older generation.

I sneak through their rehearsal,
Pastrami-sandwich-French-fry-lunch
wicking through my bag.

The flock of hungry students
bleat with vegan indignation.

Gargoyle Clinging to Weakened Towers

Reach to drink the sacred wine
and say a prayer.
Flooding waters will also baptize
the poor with the privileged.

Minarets stand over deserts
where a passionate rebellion
will eventually begin.
In European villages
steeples will rise above indecisive air
of the Common Era.

Holy Roman Bishops
spill the wax of arcane candles
with degrading dominance.
Under purple light,
crestfallen parishioners genuflect,
break bread and devour
losing prophecies. They greet
a new world's vernacular
of connectivity and appletinis.

Divine Eastern Clerics,
five times devout,
struggle past God's will.

Fifty-thousand-kilowatt preachers
meet on the ball fields of Babylon
to play the game of fundamentalism.

Drink to quench your aging thirst.
Judgment won't come
from flesh.

Oceanic Worship

    On the slip-face shore,
Pilgrim slides on dunes
        trudging over driftwood and thistle.

    Amber-tainted background
silhouettes rucksack-toting figure
strides mounds of silt and seaweed.

Piles of decomposing kelp
scent the flame-lit sunset
        flies animate grainy shore.

    The jade waves
heave like an ailing stomach
saltwater sprays absolution.

Ministers in rubber suits
follow current, crevice, and cavern,
        in search of bottom dwellers to convert.

    The ancient shanty echoes
stories from captains and fishermen
of harpoon scars on maritime leather.

Seabirds chiseled on sunset rays
reflect in the Pilgrim's wistful eyes
        like the monstrance of veneration.

    Stars exposed in the black
waves crash hard, decreasing shoreline,
evening winds wail in a variable pitch.

Pilgrim, stalwart and pure,
stands puny against roiling depths,
        tousles like a sprig in spiteful winds.

    Sure in his footing,
Pilgrim waits interment
        from a final, graveling wave.

Round-Shouldered Dreadnought

His eyes reflect
her tobacco sunburst skin,
smoky-throated vocals image clouds,
seagulls echo through
the Sitka wood of Alaska.

Spruce-scented rhymes,
melancholy vantage,
diminished 5ths of whisky
drown hammered thumps,
bellowing thunderstorm cadence
through her sonorous canyon.

He gently reaches around
her slender nodular neck,
trebled fingers hammer
brass nickel chords,
harmonics multiply,
she rests.

Manipulating every phrase
of her rapturous choir,
fondling her total breadth,
his arm brushes against her pearled curve.
With undertone of disappointment
he puts her back in her velvet-lined case.
He is just a little off beat,
not worthy to play her.

Two Doves Alight on a Dead Walnut Tree

The branches of this tree are fragile.
A flimsy roost, may be okay
for sparrows and finches,
but I'd rather be next door,
on the strong eucalyptus tree
in the neighbor's evergreen backyard,
shaded from the hazy glare of summer.

The ground below these rotting branches
has scarce pickings,
useless twigs, no edible seeds;
just a patch of dry grass.
My mate-for-life finds
the refuse of this barren land
interesting. His beak closed and somber,
he surveys the property of a human,
who would keep a dead tree
to rot.

I am ready to fly next door
to scavenge for sustenance,
but the love of my life tells me:
"If we wait long enough
grains will scatter with the wind."
I could eat, "well enough from that booty."

My reflective partner poses in existential thought.
I feel no wind, nor see any seeds for feed.
Suddenly, the branch below my contemplative spouse starts
to quiver from squirrels playing tag.
He flaps to me. "Maybe there is something
interesting to ponder next door after all."

Of course, I am ready to fly,
but I must wait
while my husband adjusts his feathers,
takes a longing look
through filtered smog
at the dry and brittle grass
we once called home.

"Fine," I coo and fly up to the power lines,
away from the dead branches.
I hope that old pigeon is ready to lift
and avoid the fall that comes
when dry wood snaps.

Under a Murders' Watch

Crow-saturated neighborhood
power poles pine trees
singular birds swirl skies
contrails cross paths

Sleek black fowl beak toward hidden rest
sycamores and oaks line the avenues
where children bike and skate
black strikes blue

Radiance

In the non-insulated garage of my mind,
a lone mechanic cranks a vise,
pressuring the cranium until stars
spill through my ears.
He bangs, clangs and pings
with a magic, sheet-metal hammer,
then he drills little holes,
bright shards fall onto my bed
illuminating the darkened room
before floating freeform
into the galaxy.

It's a ride to be seen,
a Studebaker Golden Hawk
dodging the flotsam and jetsam of space.
When that manic car superimposes the sun,
it looks luminous for a moment, flames out,
and returns to my globe
as a scorched hunk of steel.
Earth no longer needs
her exquisite beauty.

When daylight rises
I devote myself to finding
pieces of my once-magnificent automobile
and the gray matter that built it.
Chasing that daring cypher of thought,

I will scratch letters on paper
or tap, tap, tap the keyboard
with continued shades and color,
flashing radiance in the quiet
morning air.

Blankets or Dark

I am never sure if those are blankets over my head
or if the darkness has swallowed me whole.

I am waiting for a letter of recommendation
to rapture—I've heard they have a great party in paradise.

When the wormhole opens, may I be transported
to a pleasant climate, full of awareness and sense.

Orange Horizon Capped Blue at Sunset
For Michelangelo Antonioni

Clouds
turn purple
in the gloaming
of western skies.
Slow ride home.
Jealous-minded,
without a guess
of why.
Bird crap drops
on windshield
like
What else is new?

Horizon steady.
Warmth continues
as shadows meld to dark.
Driving by the tennis court
ball lobs high.
A shutter clicks
freezing time.

Schwinn Cruiser

Foster Grants
follow
sea foam
beach ball
yellow-billed gulls
under
Irving Berlin
skies.

Thin black
rubber
buzzing
S-curve
tire treads dodge
paleontological
rock
weathered
wood chips
coastal tar
scattered soil
forever together
chewing gum.

Glide along
boardwalks
pizza and fries waft
popsicle-stained
children cry.

Laughing tan
spaghetti strap
squeals

roller skating
reverie.

Coconut
butters
string
bikini
silhouettes

The feel
is naked
super tanned
Bermuda shorts
on summertime
Schwinn.

Nichols Canyon

Jacaranda and
birds-of-paradise tango
as I motor down
this prosperous
gorge

    calculating
mortgage payments.

Boxed hedges border
properties of mint green stucco
where circular driveways
park Bentleys and Porsches

hanging elms
shade silver streets
of embarrassingly large
reserves.

My busted-up Corolla
      drives courteously
      through Nichols Canyon,
careful not to leave skids
or mud marks
on her roadside canvas.

Railroad Ties

Rain
Arrives
Insouciantly
Late

Road-weary
Overnight steerage companions
All receive blessings
Diesel pistons fire absolution

Talisman rosaries tightly wrapped
Inside
Eyes of
Salvation

Email from the Dead

Word-sprinting specter
unreadable fonts
my hands absorb
the organic goop
of Marley
Janis
or Caspar

I can only feel your insight
in continuation of our shared
endeavor.

In the opaque night
my screen saver
flutters and glows
with the radiating corpse
in the presence
of its own demise.

Thunder Clash Nightmare

Extended thunder
wakes you from a sleep
of sonic booms and riptides
torrents of unprecedented calamity
feet squish through slimy waves of terror
soles rip on rocks, boat fragments float above you
helpless like ships in a Gulf Coast squall
oversized gills and scales swim
in chase.

Eyes
for Thomas Faed

Many inhabit space
on the universal canvas
while Miles blows
So What.
I peck keyboard
letters into words
with a half-painted canvas
in the room.
An orphaned child:
sad eyes looking back,
tendering rage,
softening the madness

I am glad
not to carry
the injury
in those
eyes,
across a room
locked to mine
long deep
lost
not alone, but not
hopeful

Lovely
girl, draped in crepe,
precocious
boy, confined in wool,
eyeballs glint
in orange
matte
and colorless.

Rainy Afternoon Music:
Carly Simon/Abraxas, 1972

El Niño snare drums
splatter a towered college campus.
Scrambled eggs, burnt toast,
the blackened kettle shrieks.

Clumsy student bodies shake breakfast crumbs
off the dormitory sheets.
Thai stick Patchouli passion
fills the delinquent afternoon.

Karen's Kansas City smile betrays
the icon-rejecting feminista
he met during modern European history:
she despairs that *it's hard to stay ideal
so far from home.*

His undressed altar boy breaks
into the sacramental wine,
blaspheming virtue
with Emil Sinclair angst,
Holden Caufield stereotype,
beer-guzzling, hashish-choking,
12-string hippie, on his way to
Rabbit Run.

Stacked vinyl clatters and pops
during her teacup interlude,
he rages fanatic
playing the Red Mountain jug
like Gabriel's call to judgment.
She nurses his red wine hangover,
sweet idyll flowing effervescent.

Worshiping *singing winds, crying beasts*
and Karen's spell
of proverbial silver linings…

He finds himself on the back end of
a black out
holding his head and muttering

Oye!

After *Invasion of the Body Snatchers*

She wears my wife's apron,
but her meatloaf
is without flavor,
and though the 1956 screen-police
will not let us make love,
I assure you
she no longer possesses passion.

In a village demolished by fear,
citizens look vacuous
with an undercurrent of mean.
Parties are sedate affairs
of finger sandwiches and fruit punch.
Even the Catholic parish has relinquished
golden vestments for Geneva drab.

Barbers play crossword puzzles
because hair no longer grows,
faces never shadow.
Beauticians drink tea,
since makeup never smudges.
Maids read old comic books,
as glass never spots from rain.

Policemen in pursuit do not use sirens.
There are no heroic measures for gunshots.
The wounded just bleed to death.

Downwind from a Man Sleeping in His Own Puddle

Lipsticked cigarette butts
high-roller cigars
spent condoms
green shards
from a broken jug
of apple wine
wait with me
for the traffic light
to change.

On a bus bench lay
a pile of threads and bones.
The stale smell of urine
makes me fear the post-dawn chill.
Vagrants will rise to beat me,
rob me of charge cards, ring, wristwatch
and thirty-two dollars cash.

But the drifter sleeps alone, he snores.
Low winds waft his stench my way.
Detached leaves
scatter over the sidewalk.
I arrest my fright.

The signal changes.
I look at my ring and watch,
hold my wallet close.
Perhaps these possessions
are all that stand between me
and the beggar's bench.

Singing Half-Songs by the Sea

Heron gulls stagger
through gusts and garbage
in clouds almost green
like uncut peridot.

On the esplanade, sand swirls high,
batters my face,
rotting timber shreds at my feet
on a deck in need of new stain.

A scruffy, orphaned dog
finds an equally tatty wicker chair
and beckons me aboard
an abandoned mariner's porch.

Fog makes guitar strings go flaccid.
I play boldly out of tune,
the dog howling along,
thick air muffling our verse.

I could stay beachside all day
with my shabby chorus,
tuning and retuning
in service of unfinished songs.

Scattering birds spin and glide
like quarter-notes inscribing diminished chords
on gloomy skies.

Tempest

Small vessels rise, fall,
splinter on pinnacles
of Prospero's wave.
Heavens burst white lighting,
squalls fold battalion sails,
seabirds push against
pulverizing winds.
Channel Islands crumble
from unwitting spells
cast by a mad governor.

Weathered dinghies rock
on heaving green seas.
Antonio buckets water
time after time, to exhaustion—
our only escape
is to let him drown.
On higher ground,
drenching-rain soils trousers
and compassion too.

In the wicked mood of the after-storm
Ferdinand implores Miranda,
I will need you to hold my hand.
Tsunami warnings make no sense
when guideposts
have already fallen flat.

Hitchhiking Through Fire and Rain

Downpours refresh the haze
of woodland trauma.
Singed bark, blackened wildflowers
drown from the flash of deluge.

Hail pounds my mottled boots,
as gloom hovers over rainy doldrums.
The route ahead is messy.
Cows moo discontent.
I jangle my rucksack
and bones of malnourishment.

Drips from metal awning,
a worn-torn farm,
I watch the swing
of a whitewashed gate.
I scoff a lunch of stale bread
and moldy cheese.

Earth shakes from the torque
of an 18-wheeler.
The driver slows
to scoop up my package of humanity
into his haven of a cab.
We carry on through tortured acreage,
with its acrid smell of decay,
toward a slivered sunset
on a long foggy road.

Contrition

I left what should have been said
by the side of your desk
on a wrinkled page.
A half-apology,
three-quarters of a resignation.
I left with no tears
and drove home.

Wood fires and bark of the canyon
smelled like pencils—
number two lead and yellow paint—
blade-curled wood
sharpened by schoolchildren.
A back-slap across the lip stings
like a penalty,
my tires screech over
asphalt covered with bougainvillea.

Journeys

*The Impatient Explorer invents a box
in which all journeys may be kept.*

— Kenneth Patchen

Never seen so many stars,
except in the desert night,
where winds rattle sage
and coyotes roam freely.

Earth's waxing satellite hovers.
Her yellow hue breaks through wires
and branches to command my road trip
on balding tires over crusty roads.

I am hunger on the run.
Loved ones worry that my insouciance
will leave me cold
as I continue my wanderlust.
The next county is a pipe dream.
The trip back a trudge.
Tenuous tires and loose exhaust pipes
bump along an unbroken road.

I would rather be hanging out
on my favorite city block
under amber lamplights and high-rise ledges,
at home with the nighthawks
who absorb my body
and leave a restless mind.

The journey is fading
like an unknown alley
like a shadowed crater
like a dark country road.

Tossing about my furrowed bed
alongside the grace of a woman
who could be my redemption.
Reaching to the distressed sky
sleep becomes another
failure in the night.

Storms of Change, Squalls of Pestilence

Stranded in the underworld of mediocrity,
I found her hiding in my pocket,
hiding from abandoned tenement of infancy.

I wept for her, cherished her, cared for her,
together we huddled as warriors against fear,
under stone walls that collapsed
from a Jihad of pressure.

Storms of change, squalls of pestilence.
Bells ring for mercy only half the time,
leave the kind of scars that only pride can realize
in the pressure of a hot kitchen
where frogs boil when they don't jump.

Hawaiian Urban Dusk

Darkness
falls late.
Blue fades
to black silhouettes:
    palm fronds
    rooftops
    power lines.

Flowering cologne
coagulates
in ocean mist,
settles on hired automobiles
and island-rusted sedans.

Warmth brushes face
like a blanket of orchid.

Slack Key
Hawaiian Cowboy Music

Brocaded guitar
chords
catgut and steel
ring and chime
wind on glass
fingered notes splay
bright denotations
harmonics
ping.

Bass thump
gently counters
Polynesian hip—
Slack Key
a soul massage
on
deep red earth
palm fronds finger
clouded skies
where ocean
joins the blue.

I Guess It's Too Late to Be a Major League Baseball Player
After Bernadette Mayer's "Essay"

I guess it's too late to be a Major League Baseball player
I guess it's too late to play any ball at all
I guess it's too late to begin a running routine
I guess I'll never join a baseball team
I guess I'm not jock enough to be a ballplayer
I guess I couldn't afford to give up my day job and learn to bunt
I guess baseball playing is just not in the cards anymore
I guess I am not suited to be a ballplayer
I guess I will never have a baseball mitt now
I guess I missed my summer-play opportunity
I guess I'll have to give up all my dreams of becoming a ball player
I guess I'll never be a ballplayer now
I don't like baseball that much anyway, although the poet Harry Northup is a fan
Maybe someday I'll throw the ball around with a grandchild
I guess ball playing is really out
Fielding grounders and hitting balls, running around the bases shaking hands
I guess the calisthenics are just too tough for me
I'll never play ball at all
Too much exercising might take away from my poetry time
Who are the baseball-playing poets?
Was there ever an R.B.I. leading poet?
Fernando Perez was a ballplayer
    and a published poet
But he didn't play in the majors very long
Lots of poets write about baseball
Thayer wrote *Casey At Bat*
Updike, Corso and Ferlinghetti wrote their national pastime tomes
William Carlos Williams wrote about the ballgame crowd
even though he was a physician
Many poets do play ball – softball, sandlot and bush
They even teach their children T-Ball
But I guess most poets tend to play away from the crowd
I don't think a poet would read a poem from the mound
Well maybe, I've seen poetry read in stranger places
So why not play ball and write poetry
I guess it would be hard to stop between bases
    when inspiration hits like a line-drive to right field

I Found My Friend Richard in a Painting from the 17th Century
After Jacob Duck's "Street Scene with Knife Grinder and Elegant Couple," c.1655

In coral tones of sunset and nobility
stand the elegant couple of Utrecht
gazing with circumspect sneers.

The master craftsman, flamboyant
in burgundy and green,
leans against his stone wheel
taking pause from the day's toil
to roll his eyes and groan
at the riff-raff cast into coppered shadows.

Darkened figures of scoundrels
hold court among fishmongers and butchers.
Porcelain-faced girls laugh,
an old woman raises her boney finger
while a crooked-mouthed prankster
jeers.

My friend, Richard,
ruddier than usual
in this 17th century tableau,
stares deeply into my eyes,
as he would often do,
to see if I understand the joke.
His puckish grin punctuates
what I already know.
The secret of time travel
must be ours to keep.

Lost in Space

I float, I dream. I am the matador.

— Fail-Safe

Is being alone a problem
meant to be solved?

Forlorn thoughts fall
like rock and debris
strewn across
the pitted highway.

I've traveled many days
while hiding quiet and still
in my living room.

Tying my shoes,
such a simple task,
beleaguers me.
How I'd rather
stretch across this couch,
than continue any trek.

My nap takes me farther away,
sun rests on my awakening,
the propulsion of curiosity
pushes far into the dusk
to follow silver-lined
comet tails.

Somewhere, life will be bountiful,
but maybe I dare to be the man
alone in a crowded room,
like a matador caped
in the arena.

The Cleanliness of Sand

Sky-lanterns flood the evening desert,
colors from the heavens illuminate wilderness.
The risks of misadventure brought me
to this alcove of granite. Once a hazard

to those who would be friends, I watch as family and
colleagues glimmer as new constellations
in this spectacle of space.
The fierceness of galaxies frightens me—
how long before I join this richness of gas and matter?

A hand I have not seen for almost a lifetime reaches
through smokey constellations to tap my shoulder.
Having survived a wasteland of recklessness,
wisdom arrives amidst the desert-buzz.

I am not the salvation the world needs
that once I thought I could be.
With outstretched branches, a yucca tree blesses me.

Mellow breeze awakens a shallow sleep.
My body stands against a firm bed of brush and stone.
Like a desert weed my feet plant firmly in sand.

Gestures, Situations, and Surveillances
After Terry Wolverton and Angela Peñaredondo

Seeking my aura
in the universe,
countless galaxies
—stars and matter.
Focus to epidermis
—particles, hair,
footsteps.

A stretch
and a nod
will not only clear cobwebs
of misperception;
the act itself
gives me pause
to assess.

Too many feelings pressure me
—a heart's percussive ache
—fires of invention.
Fingertips scorched
with larceny
refreshed in holy
    water of tolerance.

    The embryonic gesture
of Kubrick's Star-Baby
stares too deeply
into my recalcitrant
asylum.

Venus-Moon Conjunction

Venus has pulled away from the moon
on this turquoise night in the city.
Your eyes peer through the widening gap
of exosphere that protects us
from the cold of outer space.

I wonder if you also see me,
after all the years since we last embraced.
We thought our equinoxes could exist
without companionship,
so, we parted.

I have held other hands while gazing at galaxies
and have also stood unaccompanied at this brink.
Being alone seemed not a problem
that needed to be solved.

Tonight, however, this canopy of city light
sends me your smile as a reminder of those days
when a universe developed within me.

Dawn Broke

Dawn pressed against the window shades
        as conversation waned
    and tinctured passions stroked
        the tawny shadows of her postgraduate home.

Eight hours of dialogue wrapped in
        whisky cocktails
    red wine and Chamomile tea
        transcended by a tacit embrace.

First-time stories of fervor and fear
        gave way to silent gaps of conversation
    playful giggles and quiet stares
        dusty shafts of a single lamp remain.

Musty after-dinner breath
        tethers spaces between lips
    nervous deliberation hinders heart
        with each dropping dust mote.

Purple melodies echo
        reservations lapse
    into puddles of resistance
        a diamond scratches music off the vinyl.

Her featherweight appearance betrays
        the ballast of torso and thighs
    and starry-eyed comfort
        on his recumbent frame.

Smiles surge in harmony
        as skies transform orange to blue
    and bodies intertwine like an abstract print
        on the eiderdown.

Time Makes Two
After Robert Cray

Fingers pluck Stratocaster frets,
harp-like staccato chirp echoes
on a dark walk between
cold stone buildings.
Blue tenor-notes ride
the lonely reverb
of November nighttime chill.

With E-string thumb slap,
gnarled, strangled triads
tie up your gut,
like the lone-wolf cry
of a snowy movie-set night.

Leaves scatter by your boots,
Butler-bow crosses double bass,
wind flutters ears
and the conductor batons
his somber movement
of symphonic poise.

Affections disperse into ether.
Cymbals sing shrill despair,
guitar solo burns
like the hurting echoes
of a lover's name.
Horns blow like tree-rattling winds
under icy skies of sorrow.

Wintered streets
are glittered, strewn
with courting couples
who whistle in passing.
Violins and cellos arco
as tugging guitar fades
into memory.

You turn up your collar
to cold winds,
blow warm air
into prayered hands
and take another
brooding walk
with time.

The Deep Heart's Core
After William Butler Yeats

I will take your picture now
in the long shadows of this golden hour
where oak branches grow ginger
in their autumn bareness.

I shall frame your face to rest on my mantle
to see your comely gaze through expected rains.
Your eyes watch the spring rise with green sureness.
Then as summer trees begin to dry.

I will take your picture now.
Your soft speech will comfort me
when I drive a woodland road or stroll a fertile meadow.
I hear your voice in the deep heart's core.

Rainy Night House
After Joni Mitchell

Minor piano notes plinking rain fall
on terracotta tiles,
suburban midnight's blue raincoat
watching the rise and fall
of your body gently breathing.
White cotton sheets
barely expose milky cleavage,
rosy-brown nipples.
Sleeping grimace punctuates
the amber features of your reverie.

Simultaneous dreams mirror noir cravings
of a two-person choir.

Harmony becomes
restless with night sweats
of mutual distrust.
Shallow assignation ends at dawn
when afterglow fades into quarrels
of thunderstorms and door slams.

Practice-pedal dampens
yellow reflections of our last gentle kiss
before morning's flood undermines
the need to cling.

Far away in desert vapors,
melody plays against strident chords,
scoring this run from archetypal memories
of what we might have been.

There Was Never Enough Exposure to Shoot Your Moon

So wane
So small
Minus
incandescence
      without glow

Your face
inert
clouded
and blue

Tube metal
and hard glass
peer back at me

Just another underexposed photograph
bent and buried
in a cluttered drawer

A Plunge Through Ozone

Bed sheets
scattered shoes
socks
sleeping dog
sleeping wife

      Her breath
cannot repair
a broken dream

passing night persists
starshine beckons
room filling with effervescence
becomes
flickering black vortex

      rooftops diminish,
rockets propel inert bodies
above this inverted fishbowl
to wrestle with stars

      It is so cold in space

Arms and legs stretch
toward constellations
longing for the warmth of stars

ePoem

I had a dream
that spoke a fib

She sang a song
that made me sob

She was long
I was thick

I asked for a drink
she gave me sand

She wanted a pillow
I gave her a board

We walked to the sea
where we tried to cling

like bitter kelp
until the end.

Starling's Triumphant Flight
For a heart transplant survivor named Wendy

Thou wast not born for death, immortal Bird!

— John Keats

Leaden clouds shadow
the stone towers of York.
Green fields grow dim
in the breach of a tempest.
A lone starling tumbles
in turbulence
and decay.

A birth celebration
breaks cold.
The hatchling chirps;
the mother gasps.
Fatigue threatens.
Feathers slump, limp
lightning flares, defeat,
absolution, loss.

Branches twist
like arteries
to a sluggish heart.
Wind releases leaves.
The starling takes
pause.

A compassionate sun
fires slow passage
through gusts
of uncertainty.

Clouds open
for silver blue light.
Flowering fragrance heartens.
The hospitality
of this new day
brings lift to
our starling's
wings.

Oh singular bird!
Once brittle and unhinged,
flying high over squalls,
light-winged
but stalwart,
picking stalks
and twigs
from meadows
of chance,
coaching fellows
through turmoil
toward horizons
of courage.

Fly sweet bird, fly!
Dip and twirl.
Purpose and power
be your wings.

Fly sweet bird, fly!
Make your charges rise,
as cheers of triumph
echo your way.

Whiter Than Pale
After Keith Reid and Gary Brooker

Status Quo detained me
at the Eucharist line of bliss and decadence,
we bowed at the coffee table altar
Virgins and prostitutes mixing
in mutual admiration
crossing hearts and capillaries
inhaling with Pentecostal passion.

An Angel's hand grasped my arm
but quickly let go,
gasps and palpitations synchronized
in rapid eye prayer.
With a heavenward glance
her face went pale then white,
absorbing into the shag,
she spouted disjointed terror
shivering with delusions of saints
fearing flames of eternity.

Red lights flashed the doorstep
like stained cathedral glass,
the gurney clattered, cop radios squelched,
body bag zipper stuck.
Witnesses murmured incantations and lies.
Too many scrambled minds
telling the passion story
of a 17-year-old girl's assumption.

While Walking the Dog Last Evening

I saw a falling star,
its tail so long,
its head so black,
surely it must rest this morning
in a neighbor's backyard,
blackened rock, warm to the touch,
conspicuous on a thick bed
of blue grass.

If it struck like the truth
it could be the famous Boson
and if it hadn't been honest,
the prayers of many
would nod as they hold onto tomorrow,
while the rest of us scrambled
to keep the day intact.

Sometimes, what is visible in the black,
like reflected branches
and multi-galaxies of matter,
would support belief in substance,
while to others
the flickering night expresses
the Divine.

Floating

Hollow out the trunk
of a redwood tree
and launch upon broken glass.
Skim the green-blue waves
and cup the salty foam.
Watch it dissipate
like the shore you leave behind.

Lay back in the roughhewn hull,
hands blocking the midday sun.
Brackish spray cools the burn
of forehead and cheeks.
A grasp of freedom,
on the open sea.

Night arrives with its celestial array.
Continue drifting in this boat
whittled from a life of misread instructions.
Lost among whitecaps
with a badly printed map
of unremarkable stars.

About the Author

Jerry Garcia spent his childhood fearing "The Bomb" during the cold war, was a teenager during the fabled "Summer of Love" and studied Cinema at Loyola Marymount University during Richard Nixon's Watergate Era. He is too old to have been named after the Grateful Dead guitar hero but likes to think he can rock and roll just the same. These are the circumstances that inform his writing with references to pop culture and mid-20th Century history.

He has been a producer and editor of television commercials, documentaries and motion picture previews. He served on the board of trustees for the iconic Beyond Baroque Literary Arts Center and is currently executive director of the VCP SoCal Poets. His poetry has been published widely in journals and anthologies.

Jerry is the father of three adult daughters. He lives in the San Fernando Valley with his wife Becky and their poetic dog Japhy Ryder.

Author's Notes

Suddenly a Storm — On April 12, 2015, Freddie Gray died from police brutality in Baltimore. A destructive earthquake in Nepal followed on April 25. Unexpected rain in Los Angeles.

When We Endorse the Noise of Conflagration was written as a response to Jackson Browne's "The Drums of War" on his 2008 "Time the Conqueror" album.

Dog Years is true. Japhy Ryder is the alias for the poet Gary Snyder in Kerouac's "Dharma Bums."

Kids with Sides references the script pages (sides) that actors are handed for study or audition. During the 1990s, guys started wearing their shirts open over t-shirts with the tails hanging. This style theoretically disguised the paunch.

Round-Shouldered Dreadnought — The dreadnought acoustic guitar is elegant and provides a bold, rich, and loud tone.

Under a Murders' Watch — A group of crows is called a *murder*.

Radiance — *The Golden Hawk* is a beautiful and unique car manufactured by the Studebaker Corporation between 1956 and 1958.

Orange Horizon Capped Blue at Sunset — *Michelangelo Antonioni* directed the counterculture movie *Blow Up*. This movie, with its sexual content and box office acceptance, led the way to abandoning Hollywood's infamous "Production Code."

Schwinn Cruiser — The *Schwinn Bicycle Company* was the leading manufacturer of American bicycles through most of the 20th century. The referenced bicycle path runs along the shoreline of Santa Monica Bay in Los Angeles County. Irving Berlin wrote the song "Blue Skies" in 1926.

Nichols Canyon is one of several roads in the Hollywood Hills that bridges the San Fernando Valley to Hollywood.

Eyes — *Thomas Faed* (1826–1900) was a Scottish painter who painted "Orphans," a random choice that inspired this poem.

Rainy Afternoon Music: Carly Simon/Abraxas, 1972 — *Carlos Santana* and *Carly Simon* may have hit their peak during my college years.

After Invasion of the Body Snatchers — classic science fiction/horror movie of the 1950s.

Tempest was written while on a seaside vacation during the Gore v Bush presidential campaign of the year 2000 C.E.

Slack Key — The name of the fingerstyle genre of guitar music that originated in Hawaii after Mexican cowboys introduced Spanish guitars to the islands in the late 19th century.

I Guess It's Too Late to Be a Major League Baseball Player — Bernadette Mayer is an avant-garde writer associated with the New York School of poets. I accepted a poetry prompt to mimic her poem "Essay."

I Found My Friend Richard in a Painting from the 17th Century — Jacob Duck's "Street Scene with Knife Grinder and Elegant Couple," is one of two favorite paintings in the Los Angeles County Museum of Art. A prominent character in this tableau looks like a friend from my teen years.

Lost in Space — *Fail Safe* (1964) is a movie directed by Sidney Lumet about the cold war that has a surreal connection to a fighter pilot.

Gestures, Situations, and Surveillances — Poet and teacher, *Terry Wolverton* hosted a poetry contest on her *dis•articulations* website where I was inspired by a poem from Angela Peñaredondo.

Venus-Moon Conjunction — A two-day old moon and Venus visible to the side looks like a crescent moon with a diamond earring.

Time Makes Two is written by Robert Cray on his 2003 album "Time will Tell."

Rainy Night House is written by Joni Mitchell on her 1970 album "Ladies of the Canyon."

Starling's Triumphant Flight was commissioned by Janos Bene of the Barchester Mulberry Care Home in York, UK, as part of a house project and based on interviews Janos had with Wendy.

Whiter Than Pale is based on Keith Reid's and Gary Brooker's "Whiter Shade of Pale" performed by Procul Harum in 1967. It is a little-known fact that this is my favorite song.

While Walking the Dog Last Evening — The *famous Boson* is reference to the Higgs Boson particle which is sometimes referred to as the "God Particle."

Acknowledgements

Thank you to the editors of these journals and anthologies in which some poems have appeared in earlier forms:

Spillway #28 — "Human Touch"
Voices from Leimert Park Redux — "Suddenly a Storm"
A Dozen Nothing — "On the Night the Stars Collapse"
Dark Ink: A Poetry Anthology Inspired by Horror — "After the Invasion of the Body Snatchers"
The Coiled Serpent — "Downwind from a Man Sleeping in His Own Puddle"
San Pedro River Review — "Singing Half-Songs by the Sea"
Chiron Review — "I Guess It's Too Late to Be a Major League Baseball Player"
Bird Float, Tree Song — "Gestures, Situations and Surveillance"
Cultural Weekly — "While Walking the Dog Last Evening"

Jerry Garcia's Books and Anthologies

On Summer Solstice Road
(Poetry Collection)

Hitchhiking with the Guilty
(Poetry Chapbook)

Wide Awake: Poets of Los Angeles and Beyond
(Anthology of Poetry from Beyond Baroque)

The Coiled Serpent: Poets Arising from the Cultural Quakes and Shifts of Los Angeles
(Anthology of Poetry from Tia Chucha's Press)

Voices from Leimert Park Redux
(Anthology of Poetry from World Stage Press)

Dark Ink: A Poetry Anthology Inspired by Horror
(Anthology of Poetry from Moon Tide Press)

Spillway Magazine 28
(Anthology of Poetry from Tebot Bach)

I'll be looking at the moon
But I'll be seeing you

— Kahal Irving

Patrons

Moon Tide Press would like to thank the following people for their support in helping publish the finest poetry from the Southern California region. To sign up as a patron, visit www.moontidepress.com or send an email to publisher@moontidepress.com.

Anonymous
Robin Axworthy
Conner Brenner
Nicole Connolly
Bill Cushing
Susan Davis
Kristen Baum DeBeasi
Peggy Dobreer
Dennis Gowans
Alexis Rhone Fancher
Hanalena Fennel
Half Off Books & Brad T. Cox
Donna Hilbert
Jim & Vicky Hoggatt
Michael Kramer
Ron Koertge & Bianca Richards
Gary Jacobelly
Ray & Christi Lacoste
Zachary & Tammy Locklin
Lincoln McElwee
David McIntire
José Enrique Medina
Michael Miller & Rachanee Srisavasdi
Michelle & Robert Miller
Ronny & Richard Morago
Terri Niccum
Andrew November
Jeremy Ra
Luke & Mia Salazar
Jennifer Smith
Andrew Turner
Rex Wilder
Mariano Zaro
Wes Bryan Zwick

Also Available from Moon Tide Press

Threnody, Donna Hilbert (2022)
A Burning Lake of Paper Suns, Ellen Webre (2021)
Instructions for an Animal Body, Kelly Gray (2021)
Head *V* Heart: New & Selected Poems, Rob Sturma (2021)
Sh!t Men Say to Me: A Poetry Anthology in Response to Toxic Masculinity (2021)
Flower Grand First, Gustavo Hernandez (2021)
Everything is Radiant Between the Hates, Rich Ferguson (2020)
When the Pain Starts: Poetry as Sequential Art, Alan Passman (2020)
This Place Could Be Haunted If I Didn't Believe in Love, Lincoln McElwee (2020)
Impossible Thirst, Kathryn de Lancellotti (2020)
Lullabies for End Times, Jennifer Bradpiece (2020)
Crabgrass World, Robin Axworthy (2020)
Contortionist Tongue, Dania Ayah Alkhouli (2020)
The only thing that makes sense is to grow, Scott Ferry (2020)
Dead Letter Box, Terri Niccum (2019)
Tea and Subtitles: Selected Poems 1999-2019, Michael Miller (2019)
At the Table of the Unknown, Alexandra Umlas (2019)
The Book of Rabbits, Vince Trimboli (2019)
Everything I Write Is a Love Song to the World, David McIntire (2019)
Letters to the Leader, HanaLena Fennel (2019)
Darwin's Garden, Lee Rossi (2019)
Dark Ink: A Poetry Anthology Inspired by Horror (2018)
Drop and Dazzle, Peggy Dobreer (2018)
Junkie Wife, Alexis Rhone Fancher (2018)
The Moon, My Lover, My Mother, & the Dog, Daniel McGinn (2018)
Lullaby of Teeth: An Anthology of Southern California Poetry (2017)
Angels in Seven, Michael Miller (2016)
A Likely Story, Robbi Nester (2014)
Embers on the Stairs, Ruth Bavetta (2014)
The Green of Sunset, John Brantingham (2013)
The Savagery of Bone, Timothy Matthew Perez (2013)
The Silence of Doorways, Sharon Venezio (2013)
Cosmos: An Anthology of Southern California Poetry (2012)
Straws and Shadows, Irena Praitis (2012)
In the Lake of Your Bones, Peggy Dobreer (2012)
I Was Building Up to Something, Susan Davis (2011)
Hopeless Cases, Michael Kramer (2011)
One World, Gail Newman (2011)

What We Ache For, Eric Morago (2010)
Now and Then, Lee Mallory (2009)
Pop Art: An Anthology of Southern California Poetry (2009)
In the Heaven of Never Before, Carine Topal (2008)
A Wild Region, Kate Buckley (2008)
Carving in Bone: An Anthology of Orange County Poetry (2007)
Kindness from a Dark God, Ben Trigg (2007)
A Thin Strand of Lights, Ricki Mandeville (2006)
Sleepyhead Assassins, Mindy Nettifee (2006)
Tide Pools: An Anthology of Orange County Poetry (2006)
Lost American Nights: Lyrics & Poems, Michael Ubaldini (2006)

www.ingramcontent.com/pod-product-compliance
Lightning Source LLC
Chambersburg PA
CBHW020948090426
42736CB00010B/1317